The Greatest Birth

Discipleship in the Good News
of the Incarnation

smgi.org/greatest-birth

©2020 Serenissima Ministry Group   smgi.org

All rights reserved. No portion of this book may be reproduced, stored in a retrieval system, or transmitted in any form or by any means—electronic, mechanical, photocopy, recording, or any other—except for brief quotation in printed reviews, without the prior permission of the publisher.

ISBN: 978-1-716-44564-4
Imprint: Lulu.com

Content by Robert Krause
Edited by Stephanie Soares
Illustration by Alana Soares
Design by Christen Humphreys

Table of Contents

Introduction Letter   5

Lesson 1: The Second and True Adam   7

Lesson 2: The Baby Face of God   17

Lesson 3: The Birth from Heaven   31

Lesson 4: Miriam, the Jewish Mother of Jesus   45

Applying the Gospel of the Incarnation   63

SERENISSIMA
MINISTRY GROUP

Welcome to our Incarnation Study

Welcome to our special entry course on the Incarnation, one of the four essential doctrines of the Good News of Jesus called *the Gospel*. We developed this course just for you from our own amazement and wonder about the incredible birth of Jesus. The Incarnation is such a core doctrine because it happened only once, which means it was miraculous and unique. You will never find anything like it in all of human history, and nothing will ever match it in all of human future.

The best part is that your faith will grow when you explore this part of God's Good News story. Whenever you look at the Incarnation (most likely around the Christmas holidays), you should experience more worship and wonder coming from your heart. Often, it takes real effort to focus our attention around the holidays and be filled up with joy again when there is so much festive activity around us. However, you don't have to learn about the Incarnation only in December! <u>You can walk through these truths with another follower of Jesus at any time of the year.</u> And please work through this study with another Christian or two because you will more than double the value you receive when you walk together with others. We designed this course to be done one-to-one or in groups of 3 or 4 people.

One of the main questions we will strive to answer is, "Why is the Incarnation so important for us today?" We will explore how shocking the Incarnation was over 2000 years ago, but it wasn't just something that happened back then to get the story started and then on to more important things. No, the coming of God (the Advent) to planet Earth has had a rolling impact throughout history and reaches us today—just as if it had happened last night.

God designed it that way. Through the questions, Scriptures, and interactions you have with your brother or sister along the journey, we hope that you will be able to say, "Joy to the world, my King has come! My heart has prepared Him room."

May you enjoy Jesus and His grace that you will discover ahead. Serenissima to you,

Pastor Robert Krause

1

The Second and True Adam

Before Jesus came to live on this Earth with us, He was ruling with God the Father in Heaven. This truth can be a challenging thought to wrap our minds around when we consider it for the first time. When we hear from the first chapter of the Bible (Genesis 1) that God created the universe with His voice, Jesus was at the center of that creation. And Jesus was that voice. Here is a shocking but true thought—Jesus created His mother.[1] Then, He became a tiny baby and hid Himself inside her to receive her care and protection.

> *"Here is a shocking but true thought—Jesus created His mother."*

Jesus lived on high in Heaven. Yet, the truth of the Incarnation shows us <u>how</u> and <u>why</u> He came low to live on Earth. If you think of it, no other philosophy or religion talks about their supreme power wanting to live as a servant among us humans. It's a backward thought. Once you have all the power and all the glory, why would anyone give all that up? Only Christianity from the Bible shows us how much God loves us in Jesus by sending Him literally—into our dirt.

---

1 Reeves, Michael, *Christ Our Life*, Paternoster, p. 21

Following Jesus

At the beginning of the Bible, we discover that Adam was created in the image of God. *"So God created man in His own image, in the image of God He created him; male and female He created them."* Genesis 1:27

? *What do you think that means? What does it mean for you and me to be made in the "image of God"?*

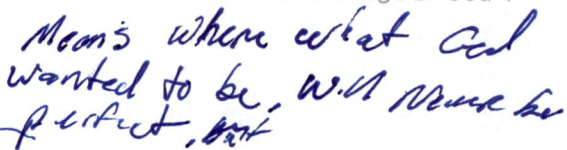

> Moon's where what God wanted to be. W.M never be perfect, but

Well, think about the role of the moon in relation to the sun. The moon is a light we see in the sky, but it is not a source of light. Instead, it reflects light from the sun. Adam was to reflect the light of God. He was the first son of God, made to reflect God's glory in the whole world. However, when Adam sinned, he could not reflect God's glory anymore because sin distorted his image. Adam's reflection was ruined.

"When Jesus came, He came as the final Adam. He is <u>both</u> the moon and sun in one man."

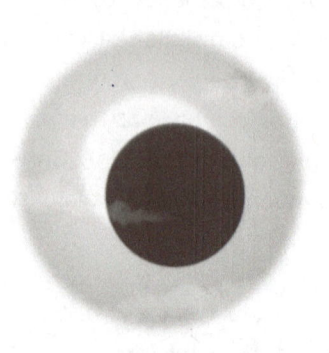

The Second and True Adam

When Jesus came, He came as the final Adam. He is <u>both</u> the moon and sun in one man. His flesh outside, like the Moon, reflects his divinity inside, like the Sun. We are going to continue with this analogy in the next lesson. But for now, it is necessary to focus on how Jesus showed us who God is when He came to our world.

When we look at Jesus, we see the glory of God.

In the New Testament, Paul says in Colossians 1:15 that Jesus is now the true image of God. In other words, Jesus comes as the true Man to do what Adam could never do—to show us, perfectly, who God is. Jesus "is the image of the invisible God," who came to show us what it means to be in the image of God."[2]

When we are born, we *are born in the image of the first Adam*. In Genesis 5, the Bible tells us that Adam had a son in his image. Look at the first three verses:

> *1 This is the book of the generations of Adam. <u>When God created man, He made him in the likeness of God.</u> 2 Male and female He created them, and He blessed them and named them Man when they were created. 3 When Adam had lived 130 years, he fathered a son <u>in his own likeness, after his image,</u> and named him Seth.*

What do you see is the difference between verse 1 and verse 3? Image. Likeness

---

2   Ibid, p. 24

Following Jesus

Interestingly, God created man in His image. The writer then makes sure that we see Adam had his son, Seth, in Adam's image—which was no longer God's image. Adam and Eve sinned and, therefore, deformed their God-given image. Re-imaging themselves, they could no longer represent their Creator perfectly. Everyone born after Adam would reflect fallen Adam. Everyone would have Adam's sin-fallen image.

> **?** What are some of the most obvious ways in our world today that we see how we share the image of Adam?

"Babies don't learn how to sin. Instead, they practice what is already in them."

---

1) Lie
2) Steal
3) Curse
4) Be Selfish

The Second and True Adam

Babies don't learn how to sin. Instead, they practice what is already in them. It is common for people to think babies are innocent because they are so cute. As adorable as they may be, they are mini versions of their parents, who are mini versions of Adam and Eve—our fallen, original parents. This sin-distorted image of Adam would continually be replicated in baby after baby *until—and only when*—a new son of God would be born. This perfect Son was Jesus—sent to us from our Heavenly Father. All who believe and receive Jesus also receive the Heavenly Father (as Adam's children received his image). They are made as "new creations" and display the image of the true Man, Jesus.

"As children of God, Christian believers begin to share in the family resemblance as the Heavenly Father grows us more into the image of our Heavenly brother—Jesus."

As children of God, Christian believers begin to share in the family resemblance as the Heavenly Father grows us more into the image of our Heavenly brother—Jesus. You can see this illustrated naturally in our world today. *Have you ever noticed how much babies change as they grow in their first weeks and months?* After a few months, they often look very different from when they were newly born. The more they grow, the more they take on the resemblance of their parents and siblings. This concept is similar to how it is to grow in Jesus—through faith. Dear Christian, know that God is making a masterpiece of Jesus in you. He is growing you to resemble His Son, and He will complete the work He has begun. Be encouraged! Do not ever give up or become indifferent to God in your life. You will

Following Jesus

experience dry and challenging times, but know that in Jesus, you will never be alone.

---

*"For we are his **workmanship**, created in Christ Jesus for good works..." Ephesians 2:10*

*"And I am sure of this, that he who **began a good work in you will bring it to completion** at the day of Jesus Christ." Philippians 1:6*

*"For we are God's fellow workers. **You are God's field, God's building.**" 1 Corinthians 3:9*

? *How patient of a person are you? Do you think you are patient with God?*

? *According to Philippians 1:6 in the verses above, how long will our Heavenly Father take to form you into His masterpiece?*

The Second and True Adam

> *How can you tell that He has already started this work in your life? How has He been "re-making your image?"*

Now, take another look at Genesis 5:3. "When Adam had lived 130 years, he fathered a son in <u>his own likeness, after his image</u>, and <u>named him Seth</u>." However, look at how verse three changes for people who follow Jesus today: "When the Holy Spirit had been restoring people to God for over 2000 years, God created a new child in the likeness of His Son Jesus, and named him (or her) ***you.***"

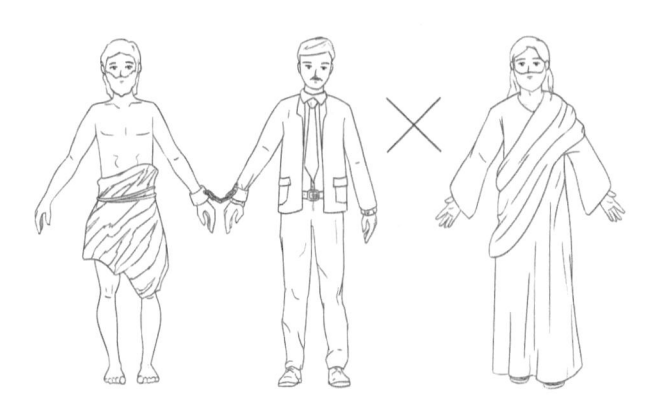

However, for those that reject Jesus, they are bound to the first Adam and will look more like him and his first son, Cain. If you've never read or heard about Cain, you can find him in Genesis 4.

Cain was known for his independence and being, what we might describe today, "a rugged individualist." He was a defiant person. Adam disobeyed God and then hid, but Cain disobeyed God and went about his business as if nothing happened. And even after God gave him a warning, Cain was hell-bent and killed his brother in a jealous rage. Can you see the image of Adam (the image of sin) becoming worse and worse? Without Christ, we don't grow into better and better people. The law of sin takes us in the opposite direction.

"Without Christ, we don't grow into better and better people. The law of sin takes us in the opposite direction."

People think they are independent beings who choose their destiny—just like Cain. We do not consider that our destiny was chosen for us before we were even born, proven by the simple fact that we are *born into Adam and Eve*. However, remember and be encouraged that the way of salvation was also provided for us before we were born. That is why it is so essential to study and know the Incarnation of Jesus.

In 1 Corinthians 15:22, Paul says, "In Adam, all die." Why? Because we are made in his broken and distorted image and likeness. Who can come and heal us? The final Adam.

Mike Reeves said it so well: "Have you ever noticed that when Paul writes of Adam and Christ, he writes as if they were the only men in the world, as if no others existed? That was the big

The Second and True Adam

picture of humanity for Paul—Adam and Christ are <u>the two men</u>: the heads of the old and the new human race."[3]

"That was the big picture of humanity for Paul—Adam and Christ are <u>the two men</u>: the heads of the old and the new human race."

The Incarnation was crucial. Without the Incarnation, we would always reflect the distorted image of the first Adam. There would be no hope! But the day Jesus was born was the day a new, true Son—who loved and obeyed perfectly—opened the way to the Heavenly Father to free us from the image of sin and death.

> *How have you seen Jesus "change your image" to reflect the Heavenly Father from what it was before you knew Jesus? Try to list at least three changes.*

---

[3] Ibid, p. 29

Look Again

In this first lesson on the Incarnation, we saw that:
- Jesus lived in perfect Heaven and came "down" into the darkness to become a man—the opposite story of every world religion and philosophy.
- Jesus is humanity on the "outside" (His body) and divinity on the "inside" (His spirit).
- The body of Jesus and all He did reflects the image of the Heavenly Father perfectly so that we can know God.
- Humans are all born into the distorted image of Adam and take on his image.
- Jesus is the new Adam—the beginning of a new human race.
- Without the Incarnation of Jesus, we would all reflect the sin-distorted image of the first Adam.

2

The Baby Face of God

How hard do you think it would be to worship a God who remained a spirit and never became like us? When problems or temptations become too challenging to face, what would you say to God? Your conversation might sound like this: "But You don't understand because You're not human like me! You have all of this power and don't have to suffer like I do. You stay where You are, and I suffer where I am, and I can never be perfect like You. So, why should I even try?"

Isn't it amazing that Jesus would want to come into our world? Look at all the pain and problems people go through! Who would ever want to leave a perfect and beautiful place like Heaven to come live in our dirt? But that's the message of the Incarnation.

Jesus was born as the God-baby. Notice that we didn't say He was a "baby god." He didn't begin as an infant-god striving to become a big-god. No. He was God. God from Heaven, who wore baby clothes—for a little while.

> ❓ *Can you think of or compare anything in the world to the Incarnation of Jesus?*

Following Jesus

Baby on Board

The Incarnation did not cancel or take anything away from Jesus. Instead, it extended and enlarged the ministry of Jesus from Heaven. This is a great truth because by sending Jesus, the Heavenly Father would extend Heaven to us. Jesus did not abandon Heaven, nor was He kicked out. Instead, He <u>reached out from Heaven</u> to scoop us up so we could be with Him. In the 1500s, John Calvin said it very well: "Christ, who is in Heaven, put on our flesh that, by stretching out a brotherly hand to us, He might raise us to Heaven along with Himself."[1]

Look at this passage in Hebrews 2:14-15 from the New Living Translation:

> 14 Because God's children are human beings—made of flesh and blood—the Son also became flesh and blood. For only as a human being could He die, and only by dying could He break the power of the devil, who had the power of death. 15 Only in this way could He set free all who have lived their lives as slaves to the fear of dying.

> **?** *Jesus became a baby, so that He could do three essential things. Can you find those three things in these two verses above?*

---

[1] Morris, Leon, *Gospel of John*, p. 224

The Baby Face of God

What a threatening baby! This baby was here to attack death itself! Do you think the devil and his demons had any idea of what was coming? There He was, lying in a manger—the death-striking, freedom-granting, baby-weapon of God.

A few verses later, the writer of Hebrews says this in 2:17-18 from the New Living Translation:

> *17 Therefore, it was necessary for Him to be made in every respect like us, His brothers and sisters, so that He could be our merciful and faithful High Priest before God. Then He could offer a sacrifice that would take away the sins of the people. 18 Since He Himself has gone through suffering and testing, He is able to help us when we are being tested.*

> ❗ *Take a moment to look at these two verses and see if you can find three more reasons Jesus needed to be born and have a body.*

The writer of Hebrews tells us that God needed to take on a body. By doing so, God came near and loved us. In taking on a body of flesh and blood, God didn't remain at a distance and throw us some occasional help and luck when we needed it. No. He loved us by becoming one of us!

Following Jesus

We all need freedom from sin. Deep within, we all ache for freedom from the slavery, pain, and damage that sin causes—and that extraordinary baby face of God is the One who will set us free. Because Jesus is in His body, He can clean and forgive the sinful acts we have done in ours. There is no other way. What life-giving hope and light He brought to us that first Christmas night!

"Because Jesus is in His body, He can clean and forgive the sinful acts we have done in ours."

? *From what you have learned so far in this lesson, which point resonates with you the most?*

Yes, on that Christmas night, God wrote Himself into the story of our world by becoming something He never was before—human. From that point forward, He would never NOT be a human. From the moment of conception in Mary's womb to this very day, Jesus remained in His body. He did not leave His body behind on Earth and become a spirit when He ascended back to Heaven. "But why would He do that?" Author Mike Reeves shares a beautiful answer to that question: "He [Jesus] never abandons humanity...

The Baby Face of God

Having taken on our humanity, He faithfully bears it back to Heaven and back to His Father. Like a good shepherd, carrying home His lost sheep."[2]

Let's try to explain this further. Jesus lived His life in our world perfectly and without sin. Yes, Jesus was undoubtedly hungry and tired, but He never suffered from sickness or the decay of aging. Since Jesus had never sinned, the effects of sin could not touch Him in how sin impacts us. In His crucifixion, Jesus' body bore the marks of sin in scars from the torture and nail piercing inflicted upon Him. Those same scars are still there. The Apostle John tells us in Revelation 5:6 that he had seen Jesus in His Heavenly state, "... standing as one who had been slain." John could see the marks on His body. And one day, when we see Jesus face to face, we, too, will be able to see and touch those hands and feet—which saved our souls.

Because Jesus resurrected from the dead, death could no longer threaten Him. The power of the Resurrection took the human body of Jesus and glorified it, never to decay. The body Jesus has in Heaven now is not a new one—It's a renewed one! And it is fully alive and untouched by sickness, sin, and death. His body is His sign of victory. Jesus standing in His flesh & blood in Heaven today means He has conquered what kills us, and one day He will renew our bodies to be like His, too. That's what it means for Jesus to *bear our humanity back to Heaven like a good shepherd*, as Mike Reeves mentions in the quote above.

So now, let's work to apply this to our own lives. Whenever we hear and learn a new truth about Jesus, we need to ask ourselves, "If that is true of Jesus, then how is that true for me?" In the last paragraphs, we read about how Jesus' physical body is good news

---

[2] Reeves, Michael, *Christ Our Life*, p. 60

Following Jesus

for us. What Jesus did in His body, we could never accomplish in ours. However, we want to draw strength and truth from Jesus. We want to see what victory He has already obtained for us in the Incarnation and then teach our minds and spirits to operate from *that* Gospel reality. Please note that we are not looking for little things to help us feel better about ourselves until we get through our troubles. No. We want to live from the foundation of what Jesus has given and has promised to give. Below is an example of what it looks like to "Gospel" something in our lives:

> **1) What has Jesus done for us** *(e.g., He incarnated in a physical body and identified with us)*
> **2) What is true of Jesus right now** *(e.g., He lives in His glorified body and will glorify mine)*
> **3) What is true for me right now** *(e.g., my body is His temple and I live to serve Him)*

> *Please take a few minutes to apply this towards something we all face—sickness & suffering.*

> *The next time you are sick, tired, and suffering, what truths about Jesus and His body would be helpful to remember? How can these truths transform your mental and spiritual perspective, filling your heart with joy and peace instead of frustration, desperation, or even anger?*

The Baby Face of God

Best. Birthday. Ever.

No other birthday has ever been so significant or unique, and no other birthday will ever be like this one. It is the one-and-only point in time when God comes as a baby to Earth.

- The Apostle Paul said it this way: "But when the right time came, God sent His Son, born of a woman, subject to the law." (Galatians 4:4 NLT)
- The Apostle John also wrote it so powerfully: "So the Word became human and made His home among us. He was full of unfailing love and faithfulness." (John 1:14 NLT)
- And don't forget about Apostle Matthew, who also talked about Jesus' birthday like this: "Look! The virgin will conceive a child! She will give birth to a son, and they will call Him *Immanuel*, which means <u>God is with us</u>." (Matt. 1:23 NLT)

It is incredible to think about how Jesus put on human flesh and came down into our pain-filled and sin-broken world. If He came down from Heaven to rescue us from our sad condition, <u>He must also intend to take us somewhere</u>. Otherwise, Jesus' arrival would not make any sense. Where is Jesus going, and why is He doing all of this?

Following Jesus

In the Incarnation, baby Jesus came down to us. Yet, through the rest of the Gospel story, baby Jesus is going UP. He is the Baby King who will bear all of our trouble, pain, and sadness on the Cross. Jesus will, then, become the Risen King returning to Heaven to take His throne. He is the Savior, who will renew our lives so that we will become Heavenly like Himself. We can see God's story and His grace more fully by looking first at the baby face of Jesus on Earth. Once we understand why He came and where He was going, we have a better picture of who our King in Heaven is because Jesus on Earth allows us to gaze upon the face of our King in Heaven.

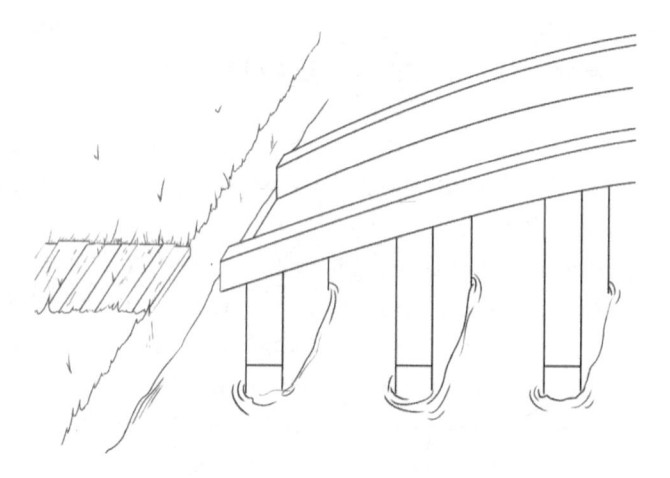

Before that first Christmas night, there was no bridge between God's world and ours. Take a moment to imagine a bridge being built over a body of water to connect two distant shores. As the bridge nears completion, there is an extraordinary moment when the two sides touch. Jesus is the ultimate connection point. In His body, Heaven and Earth touch, and the bridge connects two worlds. One is perfect. The other is not.

The Baby Face of God

What does this connection do for us today? One thing is that it allows us to be on the receiving side of God's incredible grace. Another blessing is that it removes the pressure of personal performance. We don't have to build a bridge to God to achieve a spiritual status or meet God halfway through our efforts. Because Jesus became a man, we no longer have the burden of becoming divine through self-achievement or controlling and directing our lives. Instead of striving to become a god, we have access to the God who became one of us.

Look at how these verses in Hebrews show us Jesus is the bridge to God:

> "So then, since we have a great High Priest who has entered Heaven, Jesus the Son of God...let us come boldly to the throne of our gracious God. There we will receive His mercy, and we will find grace to help us when we need it most." (Hebrews 4:14,16 NLT)

Based on these verses, what right do we have to come before God?

How and when are we supposed to come to God's throne?

How does God promise that He will answer?

Following Jesus

The Grace in the Face

In our first lesson, we talked about how Jesus is like the moon and the sun together in one person. His body is like the moon, reflecting His divinity, as does the sun. But, what happens when the moon and sun come together in the sky?

> **?** *Have you ever seen a solar eclipse? If so, where were you, and what did you feel? How did you view the eclipse?*

When we view a solar eclipse, we usually look at it indirectly using special glasses or through a hole in another object. To see the eclipse itself, we must wait for the moment when the moon completely covers the sun. What we see is a dark circle with radiant light all around it. However, if we were to look at the sun's bright radiance directly, we would go blind.

The Baby Face of God

Similarly, if Jesus came without putting on His body, He would have been ablaze with glory and judged us in our sin—with death. We could have never resisted it. The Bible tells us that no man can look directly at God and live because God's holiness judges him instantly.

When Moses asked to see God's glory in Exodus 33, here is how God responded:

> 18 Moses said, "Please show me your glory." 19 And He said, "I will make all my goodness pass before you and will proclaim before you my name 'The Lord.' And I will be gracious to whom I will be gracious, and will show mercy on whom I will show mercy. 20 But," He said, "*you cannot see my face, for man shall not see me and live.*" 21 And the Lord said, "Behold, there is a place by me where you shall stand on the rock, 22 and while my glory passes by I will put you in a cleft of the rock, and *I will cover you with my hand* until I have passed by. 23 Then I will take away my hand, and you shall see my back, *but my face shall not be seen.*"

When Moses returned to the people from talking with God, his face shone so brightly that no-one could look at him without hurting their eyes. And that happened after Moses *only spoke with God!* If Moses had seen God, he would have been ashes.

However, look at the book of John, chapter 1 in the New Testament, and read what John writes about seeing God:

> 14 *And the Word became flesh and dwelt among us,* and *we have seen His glory,* glory as of the only Son from the Father, full of grace and truth... 16 For from *His fullness* we have all received, grace upon grace. 17 For the law was given through Moses; grace and truth came through *Jesus Christ.* 18 No one

Following Jesus

has ever seen God; the only God, who is at the Father's side, <u>He has made Him known</u>.

? *From these verses and in your own words, what do you think John is saying about seeing God directly?*

Jesus' flesh acted as a curtain or a veil (like the moon in front of the sun), <u>shielding us from</u> His divinity's direct light so that we could <u>look at God</u>. This veil was an act of God's grace to us. Then, as Jesus was teaching and doing miracles, He was giving us a glimpse of God's majesty and glory behind His flesh—a glimpse of what was on the inside, coming out through His words and works like rays of glory and power.

Imagine if Jesus had come to us only as a spirit and not in His body. We would have never survived His holiness. An author

The Baby Face of God

named T. F. Torrance put it this way: "The very humanity of Christ is the veiling of God...so God draws near to us under that veil to reveal Himself, and save us...[3]

"While Jesus' body intended to <u>shield us</u> from God's glory and pure judgment, His coming into our history, His teachings, and His miracles were meant to <u>reveal God to us</u> continuously."

So, while Jesus' body intended to <u>shield us</u> from God's glory and pure judgment, His coming into our history, His teachings, and His miracles were meant to <u>reveal God to us</u> continuously. Torrance continues: "His humanity holds mankind at arm's length from God, to give them breathing space, time, and possibility for surrender to God's challenge in grace, time for decision, and faith in Him."[4] By taking on a body, Jesus could simultaneously reveal God, His good and holy Father, to us AND graciously invite us to repent of our sins, receiving His grace.

Therefore, instead of announcing wrath and destruction, Heaven announced salvation through baby Jesus' first cry. On that first Christmas night in Bethlehem, Heaven declared that God was on the Earth. And every Christmas season since, Heaven repeatedly announces: "Peace is on the Earth and God's favor towards us in Jesus Christ, is good news for us all!"

---

3   Torrance, Thomas F., *Incarnation*, p. 194
4   Ibid, p. 194

Following Jesus

> *Reflecting on what you just read, how did Jesus' miraculous works help us know that He was the Son of God?*

> *How does what you have learned in this lesson change or impact your understanding of Christmas?*

Look Again:

- Because God loved us, He came into our world and became human. This truth is what makes the baby face of Jesus so beautiful!
- Jesus came from Heaven and reached out to us so that we might join Him in Heaven.
- Jesus was still God when He put on His human body, forever. If He wasn't both, He couldn't rescue us and have the power to destroy death.
- Jesus' Heavenly body is the promise of the renewed body we will receive in the future.
- On the first Christmas night, the baby body of Jesus was the perfect bridge connecting Heaven to the Earth.

3

The Birth from Heaven

Augustine was one of the most important early-church fathers who lived around 400 A.D. He wrote on the importance of the Incarnation and said Jesus was, "Born of a mother, not quitting the Father."[1] What did he mean? This phrase sounds a bit strange to our modern ears. Augustine wanted to show that in the one person of Jesus, Heaven and Earth were combined and connected. He was saying: "Yes, Jesus was a real human being and was born through Mary, just like each of us is born from our mothers. However, Jesus never exchanged His Heavenly Father for an earthly one. We all have an earthly father, but not Jesus— His father is God alone."

The Bible is full of signs that point to Jesus. These signs help us see and know Who is real and true, and God does this through the Incarnation. The Incarnation reveals that Jesus is <u>divine</u> and was born <u>from Heaven</u>. Let's take a look at three of the many signs God gave us through the miraculous birth of Jesus.

The first sign was what Augustine referred to above—<u>Only God the Father would miraculously make the body of Jesus</u>.

---

[1] <u>Nicene and Post-Nicene Fathers</u>, First Series, Vol. 7, Translated by J. Gibb, Tractate 12

Following Jesus

When Luke wrote the account of Jesus' birth, Luke made a specific effort to trace Jesus' lineage back to the first man, Adam. But who was Adam's father? Luke 3:38 says Adam's father was God Himself, "...*the son of Adam, the son of God.*" So then, Jesus had to be the Son of God because only someone "born of Heaven" can bring God's children **back to** Heaven with Him. In other words, Jesus had to be the new start so He could begin a new race of people. God, the Holy Spirit, had to conceive Jesus so He would be without a human father, like the original Adam.

> *"Jesus had to be the new start so He could begin a new race of people. God, the Holy Spirit, had to conceive Jesus so He would be without a human father, like the original Adam."*

The Apostle Paul calls Jesus "The Last Adam." Look at how Paul says this miraculous birth of Jesus points to the fact that Jesus came from Heaven and will one day make us Heavenly like Himself in 1 Corinthians 15:45-49:

> *45 The Scriptures tell us, "The first man, Adam, became a living person." But the last Adam—that is, Christ—is a life-giving Spirit. 46 What comes first is the natural body, then the spiritual body comes later. 47 Adam, the first man, was made from the dust of the earth, while Christ, the second man, came from heaven. 48 Earthly people are like the earthly man, and heavenly people are like the heavenly man. 49 Just as we are now like the earthly man, we will someday be like the heavenly man.*[2]

New Living Translation

The Birth from Heaven

The second sign God gave was Jesus' body itself. Let me explain. When you watch a superhero movie, you often see the main characters dressing up in a suit. Take Batman, for instance. He has a rugged, outward "skin" with unique armor, gadgets, and weapons. It's also dark, so with his big cape, it gives his enemies the impression that he is one tough bat. Well, that's not Jesus. Jesus' power is on the inside. His "suit" was a body—giving His enemies, like the religious rulers of Jerusalem, the impression that Jesus was just another human being. He knew what it was like to be hungry and tired. Jesus experienced what it was like to be hot and cold. As a carpenter, if He hit His thumb with a hammer, it hurt! And when nails pierced Jesus' hands and feet—for us—He felt every bit of that excruciating pain, too.

You see, the Gospel is not about who has the most might, but rather Who is right, pure, and true. We cannot reduce Jesus to a modern superhero because they each have personal turmoil and inward battles over darkness, identity, and love. Like us, superheroes (including the Avengers) fall short of God's glory

Following Jesus

(Romans 3:23). Superhero story-writers cannot present a more pure, true, and holy character than Jesus because they are sinners in need of grace, too. When the Lord Jesus incarnated, He knew who He was, why He was here, and for whom He would die and rise again. And He did it all with perfection. Jesus' body <u>points to Jesus' divinity on the inside</u>. Being God on Earth made Him unlike any other man.

> ❓ *Can you remember some other experiences in Jesus' life where we know his "outside suit" was human? How do those experiences help you know that God cares about you?*

The third sign was how <u>Jesus' birth points to Jesus' Resurrection</u>. There's a special connection between Jesus' Incarnation and His Resurrection because these miracles happen similarly. The Scriptures tell us that Jesus was born of a virgin. Only God the Father gave life to Jesus in Mary's womb. And after Jesus' crucifixion, only God the Father gave life to Jesus' lifeless body inside the tomb. The tomb at His death reminds us of the womb at His birth. Both are dark, enclosed, and quiet places. The Apostle

The Birth from Heaven

John includes a small but critical detail that connects the two. John writes, "Now in the place where He was crucified there was a garden, and in the garden <u>a new tomb in which no one had yet been laid.</u>" (John 19:41) John tells us this was a "virgin tomb" just like the virgin womb. The significance is from the womb to the tomb, only God the Father gave Jesus His life, and no other man

---

"From the womb to the tomb, only God the Father gave Jesus His life, and no other man entered either place. No man can ever take credit for what God alone has done."

---

entered either place. No man can ever take credit for what God alone has done.

The heartbeat of God was always to make a new people for Himself—a new race. Jesus' miraculous virgin birth from Heaven pointed to the day Jesus would begin God's new family when He came out of the "womb" of the Earth. *God birthed Jesus from Heaven to die for us, and then God birthed Jesus from the Earth to live for us.* So, the Incarnation is a sign to look forward to Jesus' Resurrection and His mission to bring people from all over the world into God's family.

Let's look again at the three signs where this birth from Heaven was pointing us:

> 1) *This miraculous birth was a sign of a new, miraculous Adam.*
> 2) *Jesus' body was a sign of His inward divinity as God.*
> 3) *Jesus' birth was a sign of Jesus' Resurrection.*

Man is Coming Up—Incarnation Substitutes

Why is all of this important for us now? Well, it changes how we come to God and how God comes to us. We don't come to God through temples or animal sacrifices anymore. Instead, we come through faith in the God-man, Jesus.

Please understand that man and God are not equals. We didn't write the story nor cooperate with God to bring Jesus down. In simple terms, **Monergism** is the doctrine in which God alone acted toward us in His grace. Humanity participated in His plan, but God orchestrated all of it. Monergism disqualifies any of us from saving ourselves. On the other hand, **Synergism** is any other system that puts man as God's co-equal partner or assistant director in the plan of salvation, which means that in some small way, humanity is saved by "working together" with God.

"God alone acted toward us in His grace. Humanity participated in His plan, but God orchestrated all of it."

Synergism is the idea that we have enough good in ourselves to ascend to God and, given enough time, we would become little sovereigns. We want God to do the heavy lifting, but we don't want Him touching the things we've achieved and acquired in our lives. "God helps those who help themselves!" goes the old phrase masquerading as a Bible verse. No. The truth is God helps those who cannot help themselves. Jesus says in the Gospel account of Mark 2:17—"Those who are well have no need of a physician, but those who are sick. I [Jesus] came not to call the righteous, but sinners."

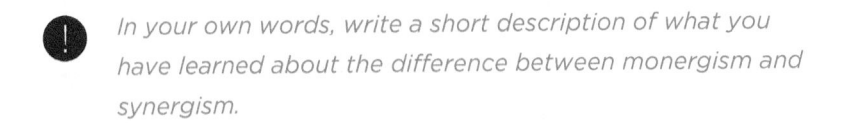

The Birth from Heaven

Synergism leaves us alone to save ourselves, but monergism teaches that grace is 100% God alone or 100% nothing. Just like the physical birth of Jesus, so our spiritual birth in Jesus is God's work from Heaven from start to finish.

"Grace is 100% God alone or 100% nothing. Just like the physical birth of Jesus, so our spiritual birth in Jesus is God's work from Heaven from start to finish."

❗ *In your own words, write a short description of what you have learned about the difference between monergism and synergism.*

You have achieved:

God Level

We will never evolve to a greater level until we reach a "God-like" status, but Evolution and "Scientism" require this belief. The only god in these theories is humankind adapting until we can create and control life independently. Darwinian Evolution is one of man's substitutes for the Incarnation. It starts with the premise that there is only matter, then man, and then man is all that matters, making God absent from the picture. Darwin's point of view is that God never sent His Son into our world to love us. In Evolution's theory, there is no power, love, or hope for us because dead matter never generates living, laughing, and loving human beings. We each have a personality and a soul because we were created by a living, communicating, and personal God.

> *"We each have a personality and a soul because we were created by a living, communicating, and personal God."*

Socialism (alongside many more like Secularism, Marxism, Atheism, Humanism, etc.) is another example. Socialism makes the

The Birth from Heaven

State the foundation and fountain of life. The State is the supreme power that controls and dispenses all the resources and gives all the hand-outs. In other words, the State seeks to substitute God by providing the solutions to society's sin problems. Any economic or government system that aims to answer and alleviate <u>all</u> of man's questions and issues will enslave the very people it is trying to help. The biggest flaw is that none of these systems can give us the spiritual answers we need for our fallen nature before God. If a thousand social programs were added to society, everyone would still be sinful, selfish human beings. Why? Because they never begin with God, His Gospel, or His grace. They always start with humanity's autonomy and then build a story that bypasses and ignores God. This is how philosophies become man's substitutes for the Incarnation. However, the Incarnation is God's complete response to man's most central and disastrous problem—the sin of trying to live in God's world without Him. The Incarnation says, "God initiated. God provided. God came down." He exposed all of man's weak attempts to be autonomous and indifferent. The Incarnation continually calls humanity to start with God and look to God in all things.

"The biggest flaw is that none of these systems can give us the spiritual answers we need for our fallen nature before God."

We have pursued all kinds of Incarnation substitutes. Technology, excellent health, and a great social status are all examples. In each case, we begin with something other than God, believing these will be "the answer" to problems that go far deeper than we realize. Then, we make those pursuits into "the great causes"

Following Jesus

of our lives. For example, there is a push toward equity, fairness, and justice in our financial markets & corporations worldwide. It is noble to seek justice for those who have been cheated or exploited through unfair advantage or malpractice. However, fixing the markets is not the ultimate solution to injustice in our world. Even if a "fail-proof" system kept contracts and corporations honest, the people engaging within that system would still be unjust and find other ways to defraud one another. In other words, we can't solve humanity's internal sin problems through external causes because corruption begins deep in the heart of all of us.

We need the deeper, greater cause of the Gospel. We cannot start with ourselves to supply the answers for our broken world. As followers of Jesus, our entire foundation must begin with God and the birth of His Son. From that foundation of grace, we can build our lives. Jesus is our *ultimate* cause. Please remember today that our loving God is the **source** of life and the ***originator*** of all good things.

> *What system or cause have you believed in where humanity, or yourself, was at the center instead of Jesus? What did that system or cause promise you that was so attractive?*

The Birth from Heaven

> **?** *How is Jesus the ultimate answer to that false promise where you had once placed your hope?*

We hope you are beginning to see how the Incarnation of Jesus is the complete opposite of other worldviews and life narratives. God is the center of our story. God came down "as a person" into our world, flesh, and death. Jesus' miraculous birth divided all other human births into two groups: those who would be born again (in their hearts) and those who would choose the darkness. Jesus said, in John 3:19—"And this is the judgment [*how God is dividing the two groups*]: the light has come into the world [*Jesus at His birth*], and people loved the darkness rather than the light because their works were evil."

> **?** *In what ways can you say that Jesus is the center of your life-story right now? (for example, are you hungrier to know the Bible more and more?)*

Following Jesus

> **?** *What has changed from when you were the center of your own story? (If you turned to Jesus at a young age, you might not remember much of your life in the darkness. So, you can ask how Jesus is becoming more and more the center of your life as you get older.)*

People who love darkness not only choose to be against God's light but also reject God's Son to represent them. They are happy to be Adam's son and to follow the appetites they inherited from him. Once Jesus came from Heaven, humanity would always face the choice to believe or not to believe in the God-man, Jesus. We cannot pretend it never happened, and yet many people do not believe Jesus, choosing the darkness over the light.

On the other hand, to love God's light is choosing to be against the darkness and practice the Incarnation, experiencing Jesus' victory. When you choose Christ, you follow Him as your representative, doing the works which please the Father. You couldn't do these things when you were under the first Adam.

"To love God's light is choosing to be against the darkness and practice the Incarnation, experiencing Jesus' victory."

The Birth from Heaven

And Jesus is not *only* your representative in life—He is your champion. Jesus went into death with His body and is now alive so that you could walk in His victorious life with your body, today and forever. When you love and obey God, your spirit and body are doing what He designed you to do. Think about when you praise God, serve others, resist temptation, listen to Him, pray in faith, forgive others, and talk about Jesus at your own risk. You are doing in your body what Jesus did, and does, in His.

Another way to see this is that Jesus incarnates His righteousness into our world in thousands of small ways, through us, every day. Paul said, *"So if there is any encouragement in Christ...Do nothing from selfish ambition or conceit, but in humility count others more significant than yourselves. Let each of you look not only to his own interests, but also to the interests of others."* (Philippians 2:1,3-4).

"Jesus incarnates His righteousness into our world in thousands of small ways, through us, every day."

Because you are in Christ, find joy in loving and serving others as He did. You don't need to take advantage of people or try to get ahead with "selfish ambition." You don't need to look down on others because in "conceit," you think you are ahead. Instead, "count others more significant" because that's the humility Jesus wants to incarnate through you.

Paul opens up a window into Heaven and pulls back the curtains to the moments before Jesus was conceived in Mary's womb, where we have a glimpse of pre-incarnate Jesus. Paul tells us about Jesus' heart and mind, His loving motives, and the depth of

Following Jesus

His humility, all of which propelled Him to come to us. Look how beautiful this is:

> "Have this mind among yourselves, which is yours in Christ Jesus, who, though he was in the form of God, did not count equality with God a thing to be grasped, but emptied himself, by taking the form of a servant, being born in the likeness of men. And being found in human form, he humbled himself by becoming obedient to the point of death, even death on a cross." Philippians 2:5-8

Take a moment of reflection and underline all of the humble actions Jesus did in the passage above.
Now, circle what these Scriptures tell you to do.

Look Again:

As we've studied the Birth from Heaven over the last few pages, we have seen:
- Three signs where the Incarnation was pointing:
    - This miraculous birth was a sign of a new, miraculous Adam.
    - Jesus' body was a sign of his inward divinity as God.
    - Jesus' birth was a sign of Jesus' Resurrection.
- Monergism is God alone acting to incarnate Jesus into the world to give believers new life. Synergism seeks to contribute or generate something from humanity into God's plan of salvation.
- The Incarnation exposes the false starting points of humanity's attempts to "rise to God."
- Jesus models, motivates, and incarnates His righteousness through us into the world around us.

4

Miriam, the Jewish Mother of Jesus

Wouldn't it be incredible if you could meet Mary, the mother of Jesus? Your first impression might be how simple and practical she was. She was not proud, nor was she demanding. If you were able to meet her, what would you say or ask? You might begin by calling her by her correct name, Miriam—named after the Old Testament's Miriam, Moses's older sister. Does Mary remind you of the first Miriam?

The Bible first introduces Miriam to us in Exodus 2:1-10. During this period in Israel's history, the Pharaoh of Egypt wanted to eliminate all the Hebrew boys from the land. One Hebrew baby boy, Moses, was placed in a basket in the Nile river with the hope that his life would somehow be spared. Miriam is the young girl who, like a *guardian-mother*, stayed close to her baby brother alongside the Nile River's waters. Miriam kept a watchful eye on him until, quite unexpectedly, an Egyptian princess (the wicked Pharaoh's daughter) rescued Moses from the water and brought him into the palace to raise Moses as her own. As Moses grew up in Egypt's royal courts, the Hebrew people were forced into hard slavery. The slavery was severe, so the people cried out to God. *"And God heard their groaning, and God remembered his covenant with Abraham, with Isaac, and with Jacob. God saw the people of Israel—and God knew."* Exodus 2:24-25

Following Jesus

Years later—with many signs, miraculous wonders, and power—God rescued the people from their slavery. We find Miriam again next to Moses (God's appointed leader and savior) at the Red Sea's waters. As God brought the Hebrew people through the Red Sea on dry ground, a new baby was born. This baby was God's new child—the nation of Israel. Miriam, the *guardian-mother* who watched over Moses, watched over this newborn nation, too—leading the women (including those who had lost their infant sons to Pharoah's evil command in Exodus 1:22) into a worshipful song of praise. Interestingly, one of the meanings of Miriam's name is "bitter waters," referencing God saving His people from the bitter times ("waters") they passed through.

Israel became a nation, and God settled them in the Promised Land. However, after much corruption amongst Israel's leaders and several centuries, there was a 400-year "period of silence" where the Lord does not seem to be moving or speaking. (This timeframe is almost identical to when the Israelites were in Egypt, when Miriam lived.)

Again, it was a time of bitter darkness, sadness, and oppression for Israel, except this time, the oppression was not from Pharaoh of Egypt but from Caesar of Rome. When God spoke again, and the New Testament opened, there was another Miriam (Mary, the mother of Jesus) caring for the Greater Moses who will lead humanity in the Greatest Exodus—the one from sin and darkness.

To understand Miriam correctly, we must begin with three crucial points. The first point is that **Miriam was a Jewess**. Her history, role, and how she raised Jesus were all Jewish. Her background was rooted in, and shaped by, the Old Testament. But the model of Mary we see today is very different from the Jewish Miriam God created her to be. Sadly, "Mary" has been so Romanized

Miriam, the Jewish Mother of Jesus

that we have *a goddess figure* who looks more Italian than Israeli. Traditions have elevated her far beyond the role God had given her. Was she a special servant, chosen by God to fulfill a great purpose? Absolutely, yes! Thank the Lord for Miriam's servant heart! However, was she the *Queen of Heaven, Co-redemptrix, and Fountain of all Creation*? No, she was not. The Bible never teaches any of those things, and the real Miriam would never claim for herself what only belongs to God. We must be cautious not to make her into something more than the Bible presents her to be, or we will take something away from Jesus to do so.

> *What do you think we can learn from the Jewish Miriam when contemplating her life, from what the Bible tells us about her?*

The second important point to know is that **Miriam was a virgin**. Yes, it was a supernatural act of God to conceive Jesus in her womb. But this act of God was because of her faith and not because of her merit. We will look more at this truth in a few paragraphs, but for now, it is essential to know that the virgin birth of Jesus was the unique way to identify who the Christ-child would be. Miriam didn't invent or make this up. God promised

Following Jesus

to send a Savior several times, beginning with His first promise to redeem us. Look carefully at how the Living Bible translation writes this verse:

> Genesis 3:15 *"From now on you [the serpent] and the woman will be enemies, as will your offspring and hers. You will strike his heel, but he will crush your head."*

The word for offspring (or seed) is the word *ezer* in Hebrew. It is a word that can be either singular or plural, depending on the context. But in this specific context, God uses the word for Miriam's seed as singular. *He* will crush the serpent's head. Who? The one seed of the woman. Wait a minute—how does the woman have a seed? From what we understand about human biology, it should read, "I will have the man's seed crush your head, Satan!" But God doesn't say that. Instead, God Himself intended to put a seed within the woman all along—supernaturally. So then, it's the woman's seed coming for Satan that will crush him—a seed that does not come from Adam.

Abraham arrives on the scene a little later in the book of Genesis. After Abraham demonstrated his faith in an incredibly significant way (which you can read about in Genesis 22), the Lord blessed Abraham with promises. One promise God made is in Genesis 22:18, where God says, "*...and in your offspring shall all the nations of the earth be blessed, because you have obeyed my voice.*" The word offspring here is the Hebrew word for seed—one, single promised son. How do we know this? Because the Apostle Paul tells us in Galatians 3:16 that Jesus, alone, was the fulfillment of that promise to Abraham, saying, "*Now the promises were made to Abraham and to his offspring. It does not say, 'And to offsprings,' referring to many, but referring to one, 'And to your offspring,' who is Christ.*"

Miriam, the Jewish Mother of Jesus

While there are many more promises throughout the Old Testament, we want to highlight one where the prophet *Isaiah* proclaims in Isaiah 7:14, "... *the Lord himself will give you a sign. Behold, the virgin shall conceive and bear a son, and shall call his name Immanuel.*" Two chapters later, Isaiah declares in Isaiah 9:6-7 that the son Immanuel will be called "Mighty God" and be an eternal king over all the world. Isaiah looks and points toward a more excellent sign and an even greater Savior for Israel—the Messiah.

Sure enough, in the New Testament's first chapter, the Apostle Matthew says in 1:22-23, "*All this took place to fulfill what the Lord had spoken by the prophet (Isaiah): "Behold, the virgin shall conceive and bear a son, and they shall call his name Immanuel" (which means, God with us).* Matthew declares that the virgin sign of rescue was fulfilled in Jesus Christ, and that virgin was Mary, His mother.

Why is this important? Because God shows us that He is trustworthy in His word and promises. His promises and signs were there for centuries. So, while the virgin birth was surprising, it wasn't unexpected. Today, many people think the miracle of the virgin birth of Jesus is *absurd*. Be careful not to call "absurd" what God has promised and delivered. Miracles in the Bible can be difficult to believe because they are God's supernatural acts, with which we are unfamiliar. However, a biblical miracle is a message verified through God about Himself. In other words, God uses mighty and miraculous signs to catch our attention and point us to Himself as the One to be trusted and believed.

"God uses mighty and miraculous signs to catch our attention and point us to Himself as the One to be trusted and believed."

Following Jesus

The third important point to identify with is that **Miriam was a sinner**. Years ago, a devout Roman Catholic lady was having a terrible time understanding that Mary was not sinless. One evening, as she and her husband read the Scriptures together, they came across Mary's praise song called *The Magnificat*. It begins with this line, "*My soul magnifies the Lord, and my spirit rejoices in God my Savior...*" (Luke 1:46-47). The young husband asked, "Love, if Mary was sinless, why would she need a Savior?" At that moment, and with that simple question, the light turned on in his wife's heart. She realized that if Mary was a sinner in need of grace through the Savior, then she did, too. That evening, she turned to Jesus Christ with her whole life and turned away from the worship of the Romanized Mary she had come to know. Instead of seeing Miriam as a sign of encouragement to turn her whole life to Jesus, the false teaching that Mary was sinless was an obstacle.

What does the Bible teach about Miriam, her relationship with God, and her role as the mother of Jesus? It teaches that there is only one sinless person in the history of the world. The Word tells us that there is only one Savior who has come. That Savior was not Miriam, but her Son. To see the truth and greatness of Jesus, we must view Miriam as one of us, with the same desperate need for God, our Savior. The moment we begin to elevate her into some type of super-human or super-saint is the moment we minimize and deny the grace of Jesus toward us.

Glorifying the mother-figure leads to replacing our Heavenly Father with our ideas and projections of an earthly mother. While listening to the message of God's grace, one Italian woman said, "I hate the image and idea of the Father because He's always so angry and mean. But the person of the Madonna, the woman, is central to all of life. I will never abandon her." Sadly, she had

Miriam, the Jewish Mother of Jesus

inflated Mary and substituted her in place of God's gracious truths. To make Mary be so very good, she had made the Heavenly Father to be very bad.

> *From memory, fill in the blanks with the three essential keys to understanding Miriam, the mother of Jesus:*
>
> *Miriam was a _____.*
> *Miriam was a _____.*
> *Miriam was a _____.*

Miriam and Faith

When you consider the story of the birth of Jesus, notice that Miriam does not go to God with the request to bear the Messiah of the world. No. It is God who comes to Miriam by sending His messenger-angel, Gabriel. Do not miss the depth of this point. The direction of grace is always God to us. God demonstrated great grace by sending His Son. And those who will receive the grace God gives are humble. The Apostle Peter said, "God opposes the proud but gives grace to the humble." (1 Peter 5:5). We see this humility in Miriam's response to Gabriel's message when she said, "let it be to me, according to your word." (Luke 1:38). In other words, "I receive and obey the grace that God desires to give me."

"The direction of grace is always God to us."

Changing direction, however, would cancel grace. Here's how: If we seek self-saving grace and we approach God in our confidence and goodness, then we don't need faith to receive God's complete favor because we are overconfident in our own. To respond like

Following Jesus

Miriam did, a person must listen to God with full humility. God doesn't give grace to proud people who feel they have life all figured out. Proud people bear an entirely different attitude—one of insistence and expectation. There are strings attached. Their approach to God begins to sound like, "God, if you loved me, you would..." This is the area of the heart where the Incarnation will have its first impact because our hearts are sadly and naturally resistant to God's grace. We always want to achieve and ascend for ourselves. We want to climb back into the Garden of Eden through those gates! But the truth is we are lost sheep caught in sin storms, and the Incarnation is God's gracious Shepherd beating down a path to find and rescue us. That's the one-way direction of God's grace.

> *When we learn to follow Jesus, we want to identify the areas where our hearts naturally resist God's grace in Jesus. Then, we want to bring those areas to the Cross as soon as we see them and learn to do that repeatedly. That is the practice of regular repentance and humility.*

> *Can you identify an area of your life where you find yourself resistant to God's grace? Remember, it might be at the end of the phrase, "God, if you loved me, you would..."*
> *Take some time to reflect and talk this out with another believer. Then, go to Jesus in prayer with Miriam's response as your own: "Lord, I am your servant; let it be to me according to your word."*

Now, please read this exchange between Miriam and Gabriel in Luke 1:28-38:

> *28 And he came to her and said, "Greetings, O favored one, the Lord is with you!" 29 But she was greatly troubled at the saying, and tried*

Miriam, the Jewish Mother of Jesus

to discern what sort of greeting this might be. 30 And the angel said to her, "Do not be afraid, Mary, for you have found favor with God. 31 And behold, you will conceive in your womb and bear a son, and you shall call his name Jesus. 32 He will be great and will be called the Son of the Most High. And the Lord God will give to him the throne of his father David, 33 and he will reign over the house of Jacob forever, and of his kingdom there will be no end." 34 And Mary said to the angel, "How will this be, since I am a virgin?" 35 And the angel answered her, "The Holy Spirit will come upon you, and the power of the Most High will overshadow you; therefore the child to be born will be called holy—the Son of God. 36 And behold, your relative Elizabeth in her old age has also conceived a son, and this is the sixth month with her who was called barren. 37 For nothing will be impossible with God." 38 And Mary said, "Behold, I am the servant of the Lord; let it be to me according to your word." And the angel departed from her.

Now, let's take a more in-depth look at Miriam's faith, as she is a beautiful example for all of us. If you look at verses 29 and 30, you can see Miriam's initial distress and fear. Then in verse 34, her response turns into a question of wonder—"How will this be, since I am a virgin?" Gabriel replies in verse 37, "For nothing will be impossible with God." With humility and faith, Miriam says, "Behold, I am the servant of the Lord…"

From this last paragraph, how did you see Miriam's faith demonstrated?

God blessed Miriam with the gift of carrying her own Savior and Creator within her womb. She didn't negotiate this plan with God. Miriam didn't give pushback, feedback, or helpful suggestions of what might be a "more acceptable" plan. No. She trusted God. And Miriam didn't trust in her strength but trusted in God's. She believed Him, and this is why God blessed her. As one author insightfully noticed, "She is blessed because of her faith, not because of her virginity."[1]

"She is blessed because of her faith, not because of her virginity."

Miriam modeled faith in surrendering to God's Word. One 8th-century writer said, "Mary conceived through her ear."[2] She heard the Word first in her ear, received it into her heart, and then the Word became flesh in her womb. Salvation works the same way. We hear God's Word first, then take it into the core of our being—our "heart." After the Word is conceived in us, we become new creations and part of God's new race of people.

The account of Miriam and baby Jesus is a pre-figuring of what takes place in the lives of believers. Notice how John proclaims it in the first chapter of his gospel, *"12 But to all who did receive him, who believed in his name, he gave the right to* become children of God, *13 who were born, not of blood nor of the will of the flesh nor of the will of man,* but of God.*"*

The Bible says that we are saved by grace through faith. But what

---

[1] Torrance, Thomas F. *Incarnation: The Person and Life of Christ*. IVP Academic, 2008.

[2] Ibid. 101

Miriam, the Jewish Mother of Jesus

exactly does "through faith" mean? John Calvin called faith "the empty vessel" through which we receive Christ into our lives. "Faith, so to speak, is the empty womb through which Christ comes to dwell in our hearts."[3]

Faith doesn't come from out of nowhere. Nor is faith magically conjured up, invented, or a feeling that manifested inside of us. Instead, think of Miriam. God utilized her entire life to bring the Messiah to us. Faith says, "Here is my life, too, Lord. Here is my story. And God, here is my heart—it's empty, please fill it!" Faith is surrendering our lives, choices, and abilities to God, believing Him to make—from all of these things—something new.

The birth of Jesus has caused faith in God and Christ to be born all over the world. If you listen to the testimonies of members in your church, you will hear how God transformed their lives and saved them; and how He made the image of Jesus in them. Each story is colorfully diverse, with past experiences and backgrounds. It is fascinating to hear and see how God weaves stories together for His glory.

You'll find that at the center of every true gospel story is the same experience, no matter where people began. In every believer, there is a moment when they believed in Jesus Christ, and then the Spirit of God filled their empty lives. That part of the story will always mirror what happened in the Incarnation. Every believer is conceived and then born by the Holy Spirit. They did not bring God down to themselves, nor do they add God to their lives. Faith simply does not work that way.

Grace comes into open faith, just like Jesus came into Mary's womb as she surrendered herself to God. If we receive the Word upon hearing the gospel—that God set His love and favor upon

---

3   Ibid. 102

us even though we do not deserve it—that is the work of the Holy Spirit of God. Faith then asks, "Do you understand this, AND do you receive this?"

"Grace comes into open faith, just like Jesus came into Mary's womb as she surrendered herself to God."

> *Reflect on the story of your life. How does your faith story mirror the account of Miriam and the Incarnation of Jesus?*

Following Miriam's Gospel Example

When you hear about the Incarnation of Jesus, how do you respond? If you think about it, has there ever been so much attention and detail given about someone's birthday in all of human history? One of the reasons God gave us so much information is so we would repeatedly return to Jesus' birth story, dig deeper, place ourselves in the episodes, and live them again. God wants us to wonder and marvel, but we don't always experience that awe and amazement when we think about the Incarnation. Over the next couple of pages, we want to explore a few of our reactions, their causes, and the model of faith and obedience Miriam displayed in her own life's story.

Miriam, the Jewish Mother of Jesus

Perhaps you are a *sentimental* person who loves the warm feelings of the Christmas holidays, the beautiful baby narrative, and the image of the host of angels singing in the sky. Please don't stop there! A sentimental person will stop at the point when they feel good or festive and say to God, "Fill up my emotions. Please make me feel good." But how did Miriam respond when she learned of her coming Christmas present? She responded to the Lord, "I am your servant." Look past the lights and the manger scenes. Faith will take you into a more genuine and deeper worship than sentimentality ever could.

On the other hand, you might be more of an *intellectual* person and find it difficult to accept the miraculous parts of the Incarnation. You might find yourself saying, "I get it. I hear the story every year." And while you know *about* the Incarnation academically, you don't find yourself empowered or transformed by the truths of Jesus in it. These are the moments you need to exercise faith, knowing that the Lord is bigger than you are and has done an excellent and miraculous thing for you. You need to follow Miriam and surrender your will and reason to God. She asked, "But how can these things be since I am a virgin?" Intellectually, the announcement didn't make sense. But as Gabriel told her what would take place through God's Spirit, she surrendered her will and said, "Let it be to me according to your word." God designed the Incarnation to be something so incredible, so out-of-the-box, that everyone (including intellectuals) would receive it with humility.

57

Following Jesus

Or you might find that your first reaction to most things in life and the Bible is **skepticism**. You want to *see it to believe it*. You might say, "Nobody was ever born this way, and our society just uses this to generate commercial activity." You are correct—No one is born like this. But that's the whole point! You would also be right in that our society steals God's story and uses it for commercial purposes. However, the problem is not in your analysis but your ability. Skepticism is doubting or denying that the source of information is worthy and reliable. A skeptic tells their heart that they know better than the source. Miriam recognized her inability to understand better than God and didn't argue back. She didn't "negotiate" a more convenient plan to fulfill her own life's dream. Instead, she asked God the simple question, "How?" We know her question was humble and pure because Gabriel willingly answered her with the next steps in God's plan for her encouragement. Miriam wasn't skeptical about God's goodness. We never see her trying to *out-think* or *over-analyze* God. Instead, we see her abundantly praising God. Miriam humbly accepted the words, signs, and child God had given to her. She graciously modeled the process of faith for us through her obedience. We, too, must practice obedient faith by first receiving God's Word, trusting in His acts of love for us, and then receiving the Son of Grace in our lives.

Do you find yourself to be an **angry** person? How does Miriam's example of faith affect you? Perhaps you find yourself easily angered by your circumstances or how life isn't what you had hoped for or dreamed. It may seem like people are obstacles to your happiness or that everyone is out to get you. Maybe you find yourself becoming angry, defensive, or evasive toward those who might challenge your plans and selfish desires. Take another look at Miriam's response to God. He had just made plans for her life. God allowed her to be chased and threatened by Herod's army. He allowed her to watch other children killed for the sake

Miriam, the Jewish Mother of Jesus

of her Son. Miriam was uprooted from her home for several years, insulted, and slandered by people in her hometown. She suffered profoundly as a mother when her countrymen illegally murdered Jesus. God told her that *a sword of pain would pierce her very own heart* in Luke 2:34-35. But Miriam doesn't seek to control the story and fight back. She doesn't become angry at God, His plans for her, or her life circumstances. In the face of all of that sudden change, what did Miriam *have* to walk by faith and not become angry?

"Miriam doesn't seek to control the story and fight back. She doesn't become angry at God, His plans for her, or her life circumstances."

Miriam had a supreme affection for God Himself.

Miriam was a **worshipper**. Do you remember when we began this lesson by looking at the first Miriam, Moses' sister? Well, just like the first Miriam who sang a new song of praise by the Red Sea when God rescued His people from Pharaoh, so too, this Miriam calls us to sing a new song. She could see that God was saving His people all over again—and this time, it would be forever.

Because Miriam centered her affections on God, worship, praise, and thanksgiving filled her heart. There was no place for anger, skepticism, intellectualism, or sentimentalism. Adoration destroys

---

"Adoration destroys the evil and ugliness that can easily creep into our hearts."

Following Jesus

the evil and ugliness that can easily creep into our hearts. So, like Miriam, when you follow the model of her Gospel faith, you will discover that you have the most significant reason in the world to rejoice. Please take a couple of minutes to read Miriam's song. And when you do, pray it as a new song of praise coming from your heart, too.

Luke 1:46-54

46 "My soul magnifies the Lord,

47 and my spirit rejoices in God my Savior,

48 for he has looked on the humble estate of his servant.

   For behold, from now on all generations will call me blessed;

49 for he who is mighty has done great things for me,

   and holy is his name.

50 And his mercy is for those who fear him from generation

   to generation.

51 He has shown strength with his arm;

   he has scattered the proud in the thoughts of their hearts;

52 he has brought down the mighty from their thrones

   and exalted those of humble estate;

53 he has filled the hungry with good things,

   and the rich he has sent away empty.

54 He has helped his servant Israel,

   in remembrance of his mercy,

55 as he spoke to our fathers,

   to Abraham and to his offspring forever."

Miriam, the Jewish Mother of Jesus

Look Again:

As we've studied the life and person of Miriam over the last few pages, we have seen:
- Miriam's name and role in the Incarnation correspond to the first Miriam in the book of Exodus.
- Miriam was a Jewess, a virgin, and a sinner in need of salvation, just like you and me.
- Miriam modeled the faith and obedience of the Gospel we all need to have toward God.
- Miriam was a servant and a worshipper whose chief affection was the Lord Himself.

Following Jesus

Applying the Gospel of the Incarnation

Now that you have completed the study of the Incarnation of Jesus, we wanted to provide you with a tool that can help you apply the significance of the Incarnation to everyday circumstances. To live by the Gospel, we need to be thinking in the Gospel. Through the Lord Jesus, the Gospel gives us the power to live a life that pleases our Heavenly Father. So, we need a Gospel lens through which to view our lives. We need "Gospel glasses." In the list below, you will find ways to see the world through the Gospel glasses of the Incarnation and will help you apply it to your life. Please know that this list is not exhaustive, but it can be a good starting point for Gospel application. Here are three simple steps to learn how to apply the Gospel:

- *Identify the problem you face*—everyday circumstances & feelings you encounter
- *Discover the Incarnation principle*—what Jesus has already obtained for you in His birth
- *Apply the Gospel*—connecting what Jesus has done for you to today's issue

Following Jesus

The problem you face	The Incarnation principle	The Gospel application
I feel insignificant	The most significant human who ever lived was born not in a palace but a barn. At His birth, He was named Jesus. Matthew 1:21. Then, God would raise Him up and make the name of Jesus the most significant name in the universe. Philippians 2:9-10.	From the moment of His birth, Jesus showed us humility and what it would mean to be insignificant in this world. Even His own people rejected Him. *Being in Jesus confers His holy and exalted name on me, which does not give me an earthly significance, but a far more important heavenly one.*
I have an illness that isn't going away	The birth of the physical body of Jesus shows our world that there is a perfect human being without sickness or decay. As He came to our world to redeem us, so He will take us to Heaven and renew us.	While we recognize that not all illnesses will go away in our current lifetime, the birth of Jesus gives me eternal hope that He will renew my spirit and regenerate my body to be like His one day—and forevermore.
I have a lot of anger	At the most opportune moment, God sent Jesus into our world. His divine plan manifested in the smallest, humblest form of a baby. The advent of Jesus shows us God is in complete control and is the Author of the entire story of humanity. Jesus is the Prince of Peace.	Many of the people surrounding the birth of Jesus had the stories of their lives turned upside-down & rewritten, yet they all went forth in joy and praise. The Incarnation of Jesus not only takes away my reasons for being angry but substitutes them for every reason to be thankful and full of worship.

Applying the Gospel of the Incarnation

The problem you face	The Incarnation principle	The Gospel application
God seems so far away	One of the names of Jesus is Immanuel, which means *God with Us*. The Incarnation fulfilled the promise that God would be near and present in our world *with us.*	If Jesus stayed in Heaven and never took on a body, God would certainly be far away. The Incarnation is the Good News for my heart that God has come near and has done for me in this life what I could not do for myself. He is near because He was born here on the Earth.
I'm not able to realize my dreams	The Apostle Paul teaches us that God's plan supersedes all other plans. *"But when the fullness of time had come, God sent forth his Son…"* Galatians 4:4. On the night of His birth, the angels sang to the shepherds that the Savior had come: *"Glory to God in the highest, and on earth peace among those with whom He is pleased!"* Luke 2:14. Joseph had a different plan for his marriage to Miriam until God gave him a new one. *"And her husband Joseph…resolved to divorce her quietly."* Matthew 1:19.	Our world proclaims that the way to a full life is to follow our dreams and that we should do whatever we desire. Often, our dreams place us at the "center-stage" of our lives. The Incarnation puts Jesus at the center-stage of history and the universe. The birth of Jesus is the good news that God's dreams are bigger and better than my own. To apply the Gospel, I need to trust that through Jesus, the Father loves me and has my best interests in mind. Being in Jesus *is* living the fullest life.

Following Jesus

The problem you face	The Incarnation principle	The Gospel application
I can't make enough money to make me happy	It is the arrival of Jesus that makes us happy because, in Him, we find all of the riches of Heaven. When Jesus came into our world, He was surrounded by the poor, even from the beginning. Although everyone was poor and in great need, they broke out in praise & song. Look at Miriam's song, *"My soul magnifies the Lord, and my spirit rejoices in God my Savior, for he has looked on the humble estate of his servant... he has filled the hungry with good things, and the rich he has sent away empty."* Luke 1:47, 48, 53.	Experiencing poverty is agonizing. Through the responses of all the people near Jesus at His birth, we see that the Lord loves the poor and makes them happy with better news than money can provide. We can also experience the agony of feeling like we never have enough money. That is the effect of the sin of greed. In this case, we must preach the Gospel to our hearts that Jesus became poor for our sake that we might become rich in Him (not in this world). We must make Jesus our new definition of wealth.
I feel a lot of darkness, discouragement, and loneliness	Centuries before Jesus was born, Isaiah the prophet saw His birth and prophesied, "The people who walked in darkness have seen a great light; those who dwelt in a land of deep darkness, on them has light shone." Isaiah 9:2. Then, in Isaiah 60:1, he writes: "Arise, shine, for your light has come, and the glory of the Lord has risen upon you." Centuries later, just before the birth of Jesus,	Often, loneliness comes when we feel that nobody is taking an interest in us. We don't feel needed or wanted, or that anybody can relate to the discouragement, pain, or darkness, we are experiencing. The Gospel is a beam of light into our souls. It calls to us to say that the day has dawned, and the Son is shining upon us. God sees us,

Applying the Gospel of the Incarnation

The problem you face	The Incarnation principle	The Gospel application
	Zechariah, a priest in the temple, prophesied that the Incarnation would be like: "the sunrise shall visit us from on high; to give light to those who sit in darkness…" Luke 1:78-79. Also, the apostle John said, in telling us about the Incarnation: "The true light, which gives light to everyone, was coming into the world." John 1:9.	knows us, and gives us a glorious purpose for which to live. Arise, shine! Your light has come! The darkness you are experiencing will never have the last word.
I often worry about the unknown or am afraid of what might happen in the future	Even after 400 years of what seemed as silence from God, He fulfilled His promise in sending Jesus the Messiah, Savior of the world. In the Incarnation, everything worth fearing dissipates in the one who is Christ, our Lord. God keeps His promises. God was faithful to His Word in the past. He worked out every detail precisely as He said He would. We can trust Him to be faithful to His Word for our future.	Although I do not know everything that is to come, I am okay because God knows everything. I can feel safe and secure, knowing that by faithfully sending Jesus, God has shown me that He is for my eternal good and His glory. I may not know the details of how my personal story is written, but I am sure of how it ends. This same Jesus who came to our world in linen cloths will come again in glorious clouds for all of those whom He has saved from their sins to live with Him forever.

Following Jesus

The problem you face	The Incarnation principle	The Gospel application
At times, I feel overwhelmed and anxious about all that I need to do and take care of.	It is a fascinating truth that Jesus' arrival as a newborn infant happened in the middle of the night to parents who were traveling by foot. There was no hospital, and they were simply trying to pay their taxes. They must have both felt so overwhelmed. In that way, God could show them that He was in control. With the fate of the world resting on a baby who was sleeping in a feeding trough, the Heavenly Father orchestrated every detail, guided every step, and lovingly gave us the Gospel in the most humble of ways imaginable.	There is nothing that falls outside of the control and reign of God. When we feel like everything is in chaos, we remember that in Him, all things hold together. Jesus came that we would be His people. *"But to all who...believed in his name, he gave the right to become children of God."* John 1:12. As a child of God, I can relieve myself of the pressure to be in control. In Jesus, I can evaluate all my decisions and responsibilities, remembering that if Jesus was taken care of by the Father, He is taking care of me too. I can work hard and do well, but I will not be anxious about what I cannot do.
What is my purpose and reason for being?	The Incarnation of Jesus demonstrated to the world what pure and perfect humanity was to be. Jesus is known as the Second Adam because the first Adam rebelled against God and was cursed. Therefore, Jesus is the true man, who, in coming in His flesh, filled up everything	Belief in the One whom God sent, and the power of God given to me, sets me free from continuing to reflect the distorted image of the first Adam. I am, instead, to be a reflection of the Second Adam and live for the glory of God. Reflecting

Applying the Gospel of the Incarnation

The problem you face	The Incarnation principle	The Gospel application
	it means to be human. To be in Jesus, then, is to be blessed and live as a blessing to the world like He did. Additionally, all who saw the Christ-child began to worship Him. We were created to worship our Creator. Therefore, the birth of Jesus opened the door for us to worship God rightly, once and for all.	Christ means to love Him with all that I am, love others as He has loved me, and to tell and teach the world about His saving grace and majesty.
I sometimes think I will disappoint others by not doing or being enough.	Up until the birth of Jesus, humanity showed itself incapable of doing or being enough in this world. Humanity always had the desire to be good enough for God and others, to re-ascend back into the Garden of Eden. However, the act of descending from Heaven in the Incarnation is God's answer to every human attempt at doing or being enough before God and others. Remember, grace comes to us and needs to be received, not achieved.	Because Jesus came down to us, we do not need to feel the pressure to be enough for God and others. He is the One in whom God is well-pleased. Jesus truly is enough. If we are in Him, then we are His heirs - having been given all of Christ's righteousness. What is true of Jesus is now also true of me. I am a person in whom God is well-pleased.

Following Jesus

> *Now that you have read through these examples above, we would like to ask you to think of a few yourself so you can practice applying and living the Gospel, too. Simply start with what you are facing now and where you need the Lord's grace. Then, see where the Incarnation is good news for your heart and life. If you find yourself struggling to figure out a principle or an application, don't hesitate to ask a friend or your discipleship partner(s) for their help, too.*

The problem you face	The Incarnation principle	The Gospel application

Applying the Gospel of the Incarnation

The problem you face	The Incarnation principle	The Gospel application

smgi.org/greatest-birth